Textile Time

Using yarn and fabrics

Marleen Morgans
Helen Robinson

Illustrations by Marleen Morgans

Edward Arnold

© Marleen Morgans and Helen Robinson 1986

First published in Great Britain 1986
by Edward Arnold (Publishers) Ltd
41 Bedford Square
London WC1B 3DQ

Edward Arnold (Australia) Pty Ltd
80 Waverley Road
Caulfield East
Victoria 3145
Australia

British Library Cataloguing in Publication Data

Morgans, Marleen
  Textile time: using yarns and fabrics
  1. Textile fabrics
  I. Title   II. Robinson, Helen
  677   TS1446

ISBN 0–7131–0956–4

All rights reserved. No part of this publication may be reproduced, stored in a retrieval system, or transmitted in any form or by any means, electronic, photocopying, recording, or otherwise, without the prior permission of Edward Arnold (Publishers) Ltd.

The front cover shows work by pupils of
St. Aidan's School, Carlisle.

Text set in 12/14pt Souvenir Light
by The Castlefield Press, Wellingborough, Northants
Printed in Great Britain by the Bath Press, Avon
Bound by W.H. Ware & Sons Ltd, Clevedon, Avon

Contents

To the teacher   4

Chapter 1   Yarn   5

What is a fibre?   6
Making a yarn or thread   8
Experimenting with yarn   10
Project 1 – Yarn collage using fruit and vegetables   11
Project 2 – Moving lines collage   12
Project 3 – Insect collage   14
Project 4 – Wriggling animals or reptiles   16
Drawn and written projects on yarn   17
Crossword on yarns and fibres   18

Chapter 2   Colour   19

Properties of colour   20
Experimenting with colour   21
Project 1 – Rainbow collage   22
Project 2 – Star struck   23
Project 3 – Collage using hot colours   24
Project 4 – Figure mobile   25
Project 5 – Camouflage collage   28
Project 6 – Collage using cold colours   30
Drawn and written projects on colour   31
Crossword on colour   32

Chapter 3   Texture   33

Experimenting with texture   35
Project 1 – Glove puppet   36
Project 2 – A plate of food   38
Project 3 – Face collage   40
Project 4 – A prickly cactus   42
Project 5 – Latchhook wall hanging   44
Drawn and written projects on texture   46
Crossword on texture   47

Chapter 4   Pattern and Shape   48

Experimenting with patterns   49
Project 1 – Printed table mat   50
Project 2 – Decorative cube or dice   52
Project 3 – Flying kite   54
Project 4 – Patchwork ball   56
Project 5 – Log cabin patchwork pencil case   58
Project 6 – Badges   60
Drawn and written project on pattern and shape   61
Crossword on pattern and shape   62

Chapter 5   Techniques   63

To the teacher

Fibres and yarns are an important part of modern living, and an understanding of their properties is of relevance to boys and girls alike. Historically, this subject has been called needlework and has been limited to girls, but with the advent of the Equal Opportunities Act and craft rotational schemes for junior pupils, it has become necessary to review the syllabus to meet these new demands.

This book has developed as a result of our own practical efforts to answer the demands the current situation has created, especially such as those imposed by shortage of money and time. It is eminently suitable for co-educational and mixed ability classes, and is aimed at pupils between 10 and 13 years of age.

It will be seen from the text that the aim is to give pupils the experience of textiles as a creative medium, and through use and experiments, build up the pupils' knowledge of the aesthetic and physical properties of fabrics used to make the clothes they wear. However, it has not been intended to present a sequenced plan of work, rather that teachers select projects in line with their own syllabus, the number attempted depending on the time available for the course. The practical projects which have been included will help guide the pupils, but it is hoped that the teacher will encourage them to design individual pieces and be creative in their approach.

M.M. & H.R.

List of equipment for each chapter

Chapter 1
Cord, fabric, PVA glue, yarns, hessian.
Chapter 2
Crayons, card, coloured fabrics, PVA glue, embroidery threads, hessian, yarns.
Chapter 3
Texured fabrics, sugar paper, coloured felt, yarns, calico, foam, scraps, stuffing, PVA glue, masking tape, rug canvas, latch hooks.
Chapter 4
Hessian, dyes, card, paper, felt, fabrics, stuffing, yarns, calico.

Chapter 1
Yarn

Men and women have always needed to cover their bodies for warmth and protection. They have used leaves and animal skins. However, the leaves did not last long, while the skins were stiff and heavy making movement difficult.

Gradually they learned how to collect the hairs from an animals skin, twist them together to form a yarn and then weave the yarn into cloth or fabric. The final process is to make the fabric into clothes. Clothes made from fabric are much more comfortable than using the whole animal skin.

Leicester Longwool showing natural crimp of the fleece.

For the meaning of **crimp** refer to page 10.

What is a fibre?

A single fibre is one hair from the fleece of a sheep, or one strand from a ball of cotton-wool. As a single fibre it is not very long or strong. There are many different types of fibres, depending on where they have come from, and the diagrams on page 7 show how they can be grouped.

Many fibres are twisted together to form a continuous **yarn**. Sometimes, fibres from two groups are twisted together, e.g. cotton fibres twisted with polyester fibres.

This yarn is then used to make fabric by one of the following processes:
1 Weaving
2 Knitting and Crochet
3 Bonding
4 Felting
5 Netting
6 Lace

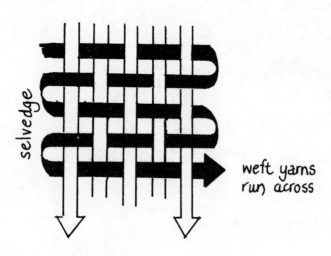

woven fabric
warp yarns run lengthwise

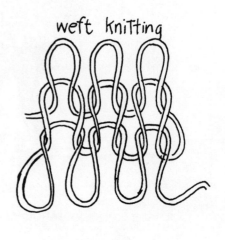

knitted fabric

Fibres

Natural Fibres

Animal Fibres → Wool, Silk

Plant Fibres → Cotton, Linen

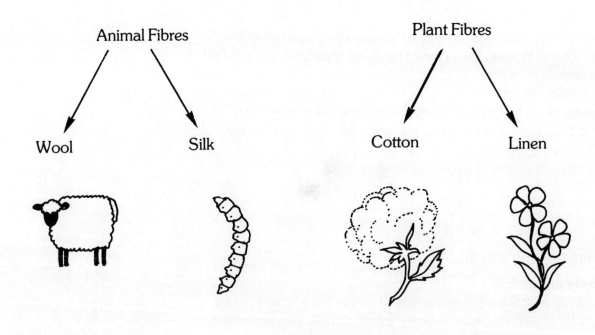

Man-Made Fibres

Regenerated Fibres (from wood pulp) → Rayons

Synthetic Fibres (from chemicals) → Nylons, Polyesters, Acrylics

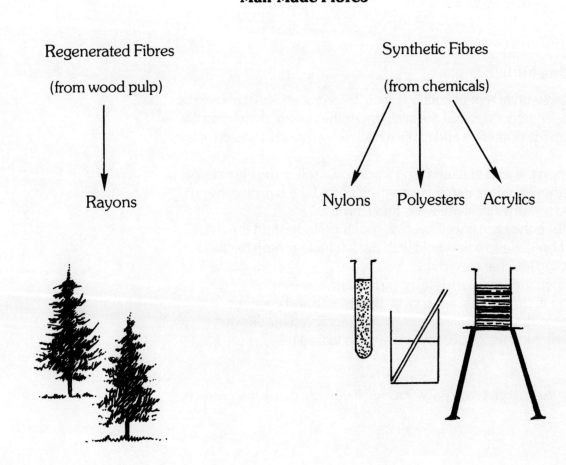

Making a yarn or thread

A yarn has a rope-like structure, and is made up of shorter lengths of threads we call **fibres**. If you look at a single fibre from a length of knitting wool you will see that it is fairly short in length and not very strong. When many fibres are collected together loosely they form a fluffy mass like a ball of cotton wool, but if the fibres are twisted together they form a **yarn** which is longer and stronger than the single fibres.

This twisting process is called **spinning.**

Spinning your own yarn

Materials needed:
Potato, twig, with a knotch at the top, 50 cm of thick knitting wool, cotton wool or stuffing fibres or raw wool which has been pulled out to form a loose rope.

Working hints

1 Start with 50 cm of knitting wool. Tie to the stick just above the potato, wind once round the stick under the potato, then bring the wool up the other side and make a hitch-knot round the notch of the twig.

2 Open the end of the knitting wool and a roll of the fibres to be spun, then overlapping the two sets of fibres by 8 cm, give the spindle a sharp clockwise twist, and let it fall.

3 When the yarn is well twisted, rest the spindle, and draw out more fibres. Keep a firm hold with the left hand to stop the twist extending into the teased roll.

4 When the spun yarn is too long for further spinning, wind it onto the twig at the original knot, re-tie the spindle and continue.
Bumps in the yarn, called slubs, can be achieved by allowing different thicknesses of yarn to leave the teased roll.

Check the diagrams on page 9 to see if you are doing this correctly.

Hand spinning

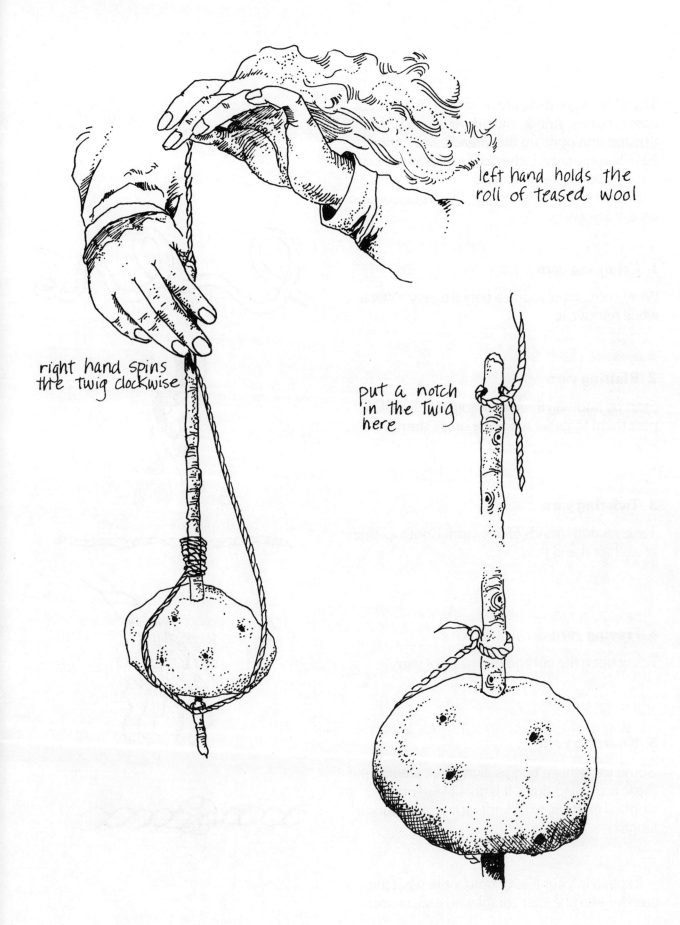

left hand holds the roll of teased wool

right hand spins the twig clockwise

put a notch in the twig here

9

Experimenting with yarn

There are a great variety of yarns in the form of cords, twines, strings, threads and wools. If we unwind and open up the threads, twist, crimp, fray, tease, unravel, chop or knot them we can create many different effects.

Collect a large selection of different yarns and try the following:

1 Crimping yarn

Wind some wool round a pencil tightly. After a while remove it.

2 Plaiting yarn

Start by knotting three ends together and then plait them together to form a single strand.

3 Twisting yarn

Take several strands of fine yarn. Knot together at each end and twist.

4 Fraying yarn

Tease open the cut end of a piece of yarn.

5 Knotting yarn

Some yarns have bumps along their length, and these are called slubs. It is possible to make slubbed yarns by tying knots at intervals along its length.

Explain in your files or notebooks what the yarn looked like after completing each process.

Project 1

Yarn collage using fruit and vegetables

Using fruit and vegetables as ideas, design and make a yarn collage.

Working hints

1 Cut some fruit and vegetables in half and do a large simplified drawing of one half on rough paper. Look at the drawings on this page for ideas, but your drawing must be much bigger.

2 Carefully select a background of sugar-paper, cardboard or fabric, in a suitable colour 25 cm × 30 cm.

3 Select some suitable yarns, thinking especially about colour. Perhaps you can use some yarn you have spun yourself.

4 Transfer the drawing from rough paper onto the background card or fabric (see page 64).

5 Apply PVA glue to the drawn line with the with the edge of a piece of card.

6 Press the yarn onto the glued line, holding it in place with a pencil point until firm. When it is finished, there should not be any fabric or card showing between the drawn lines.

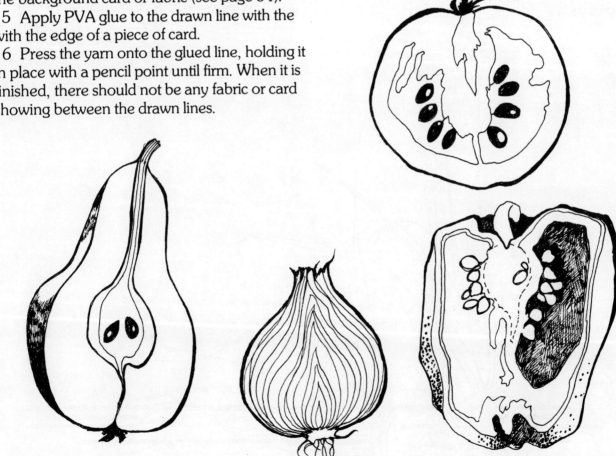

Project 2
Moving lines collage

Design and make a yarn collage to show the flowing or moving lines that occur in nature.

Working hints

1 Make a list of ideas of flowing movement that happen in nature. For example:
   a) rolling waves at the seaside
   b) trees being blown in a storm
   c) long hair being blown by the wind.
2 First sketch your idea out in rough.
3 Transfer the sketch onto a background of card or plain fabric (page 64).
4 Apply the glue to the drawn line with the edge of a piece of card, and stick the yarn onto the line. Use continuous lengths to create the impression of movement. You can achieve further effects by using knotted, unravelled or frayed yarns.

Rolling waves at the seaside

Waving branches of a palm tree

Project 3
Insect collage

Working hints

1 Make a list of insects that have interesting shapes. For example, butterflies, grasshoppers and bees.

Choose one or two examples, and using pictures from nature books or live insects, draw a simplified outline. Using different yarns which have been frayed or unravelled (page 10), show how each can be decorated.

2 Choose a different background that can be designed with yarn for your insect. For example:

3 In pencil, first draw the background on a piece of card, then add one or two insects from the ones you have drawn.

4 Glue lengths of yarn over the lines showing the background pattern.

5 Glue the insects straight onto the background or make them separately on fabric, and stick them on afterwards.

A spider's web

A collage using frayed, knotted, unwoven, coiled, crimped and continuous lengths of yarn.

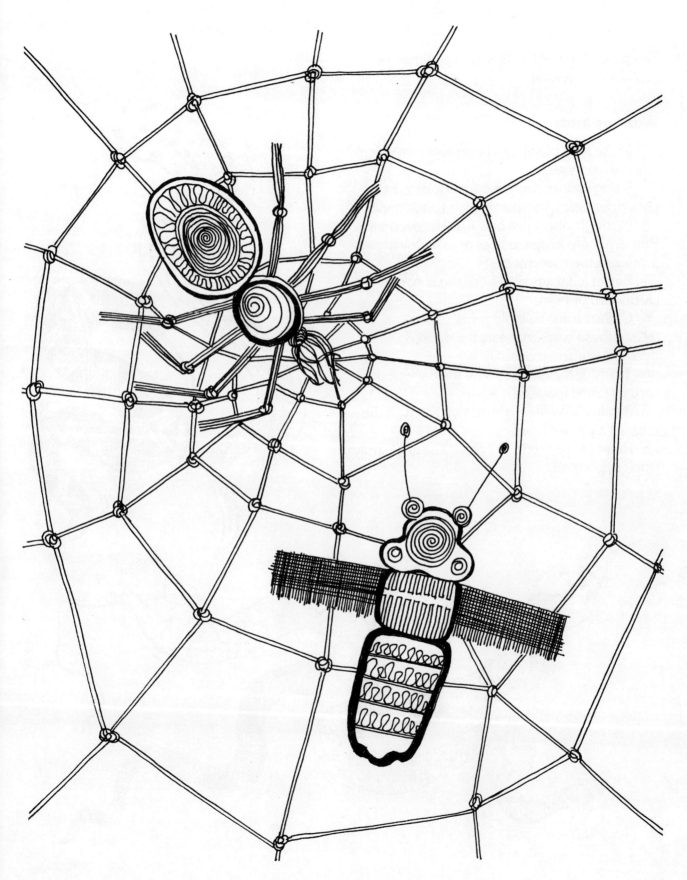

Project 4
Wriggling animals or reptiles

Design and make a collage using animals or reptiles that wriggle.

Working hints

1 Make a list of animals or reptiles that wriggle when they move.
2 Using pictures from nature books to help you, draw one large example on rough paper.
3 In rough, also show how it will be decorated. Remember to keep the lines of yarn flowing to represent the movement.
4 Select a background from sugar-paper, cardboard or fabric.
5 Collect some suitable yarns, and crimp, plait or fray these yarns to create the desired decorative effect (page 10).
6 Transfer the drawing onto the background card or fabric (page 64).
7 Apply PVA glue to the drawn line with the edge of a piece of card.
8 Press the yarn onto the glued line until firmly stuck in position.

Drawn and written projects on yarn

Read the chapter before answering the questions.

1 Write down ten words from this chapter that describe a length of yarn. Using these words write a poem with the title YARN.

2 Complete the following:
The names of two fibres which come from animals are . . . and . . .
Fibres which come from plants and animals are called . . . fibres.

3 Look at the end of your finger and on a piece of plain paper draw the lines that you can see. Using this drawing as a starting point, create a yarn collage called Finger Print.

4 Imagine that you were a piece of fleece on a fence. Using this as the beginning of a story, describe your adventures after being picked up by a small child.

5 Suggest fibres that can be mixed with the following:
   a) Cotton and . . .
   b) Wool and . . .
   c) Rayon and . . .

6 Carefully pull out a single fibre from a woollen yarn and draw its shape.

7 Complete the following:
There are two groups of man-made fibres. One group comes from pulped trees and is called . . . The other group is made from chemicals and is called . . .

8 Collect the names of as many different fibres as you can by looking at the labels on the clothes that you wear. Draw out the following chart and put the fibres under the correct headings.

Natural fibres	Man-made fibres

Crossword on yarns and fibres

Copy the crossword onto paper and complete.

Across

1 Yarn threads which are put lengthwise on the loom.
4 The name of a fabric made from regenerated fibres.
6 A very strong vegetable fibre which comes from the flax plant.
7 This happens during the spinning process and adds strength to the yarn.
8 Man-made fibres made from chemicals.
10 A breed of sheep from Australia producing very fine quality wool.
11 The name of a fabric made from cotton used for jeans.

Down

1 Yarn thread which weaves in and out of the warp threads on the loom.
2 A man-made fibre often mixed with cotton for shirts.
3 A natural fibre which is cool to wear.
4 The name of a group of man-made fibres made from wood pulp.
5 An animal fibre produced by a worm which makes a very fine fabric.
6 The apparatus used for weaving fabric.

Chapter 2
Colour

The colour of a piece of yarn or fabric is its **hue**, i.e. whether it is blue, green or brown.

Primary colours

These are the brightest, purest colours when not mixed with any other colour.
blue
red
yellow

Secondary colours

These are a mixture of two primary colours to get orange, green or violet.
blue + yellow = green
blue + red = violet
red + yellow = orange

Primary and secondary colours together make up the hues of the rainbow or spectrum.

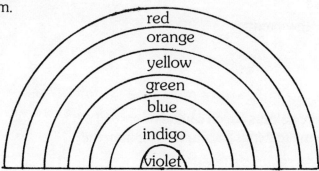

Tone

The **tone** of a colour describes the lightness or darkness of that colour. In order to make a colour lighter it must have white mixed with it. In order to make a colour darker it must have black mixed with it. In this way it is possible to change the tonal value of a colour.
To make a tint of a colour – add white
e.g. **red + white = pink**
To make a shade of a colour – add black
e.g. **blue + black = navy blue**

19

Properties of colour

What can colour do?

Colour can give instructions, e.g.   red for stop
green for go

Colour can be used for warnings, e.g.   yellow lines
zebra crossings

Colour can identify, e.g.   the wires in a plug
football teams

Colour attracts attention, e.g.   peacock feathers
telephone box

Colour can camouflage, e.g.   tiger
chameleon

Warm colours

Red, orange, yellow and pink are all colours which can be described as warm. They have the ability to make things appear bigger than they actually are.
Hot colours can represent:
    Danger signals in flags and flares
    Anger . . . to see red
    Embarrassment . . . red faced
    Guilt . . . caught red handed
    Good time . . . painting the town red

Cold colours

White, grey, blue and green are colours which can be described as cold. They have the ability to make things appear smaller than they actually are.
Cold colours can represent:
    Cleanliness
    Truce . . . white flag
    Fright . . . as white as a sheet
    Sadness . . . to have the blues
    Surprise . . . out of the blue

Black fabric absorbs the light and makes the colours next to it seem brighter.
    White fabrics reflect the light, which is why they are used so much for clothes in hot climates. Also white clothes make other colours seem less brilliant.
    Black and white are not colours and they therefore provide excellent backgrounds for textile work.

Experimenting with colour

1 Using a pencil and a compass. Draw a rainbow and colour it in.

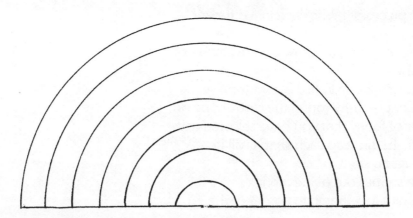

2 This diagram has a dazzling effect if coloured in using only black and white or the opposite colours in the colour circle
e.g. red with green
     blue with orange
     purple with yellow.
Draw it on to paper and colour it in. Try another pattern e.g. different sized circles and colour them in using only 2 colours.

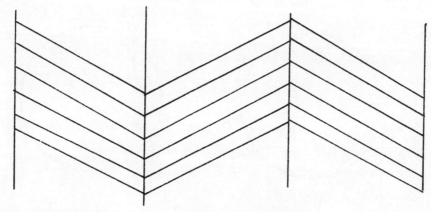

3 Collect a variety of green fabrics or paper, plain or patterned. Using a leaf template, cut out 20 shapes and stick down onto card so that they overlap and resemble foliage on a tree.

Project 1
Rainbow collage

Working hints

1 Collect pieces of fabric each in a different colour of the rainbow.
2 On stiff paper or card draw a 5 cm square or a circle shape.
3 Cut out this shape to use as a pattern or template. That is, draw round the card shape on each colour of fabric that you have selected with a soft pencil. In this way each shape will be exactly the same size.
4 Cut the shapes out of the fabric.
5 Place them together in the order of the rainbow.
6 Stick the shapes onto card overlapping the edges to form an individual collage or classroom display.

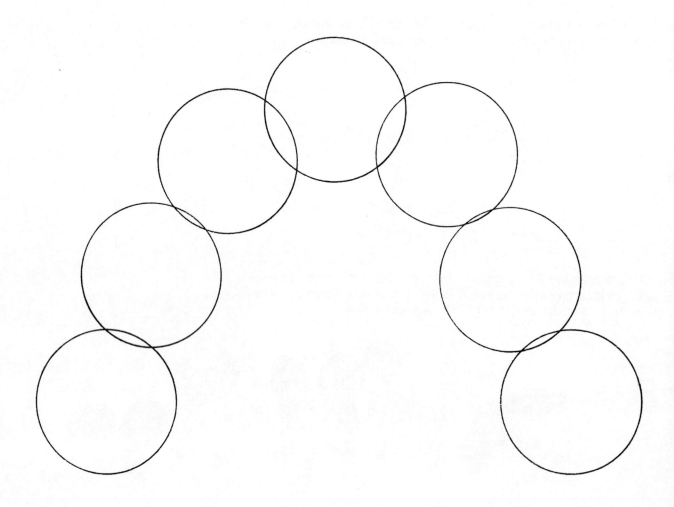

Project 2
Star struck

Working hints

1 Draw an irregular star shape on card, and cut it out to use as a template (page 64).

2 Select different materials in one colour, e.g. red. Include tints and shades of that colour, e.g. pinks and dark reds.

3 Use the template to mark out a star shape on each piece of material. Cut out the stars.

4 Assemble them starting with the palest on the left, overlapping them slightly until the darkest star is on the right.

5 Stick them onto a firm background fabric such as hessian.

6 Decorate with hand sewn stitches (page 63). In the example illustrated, running stitch and french knots were used.

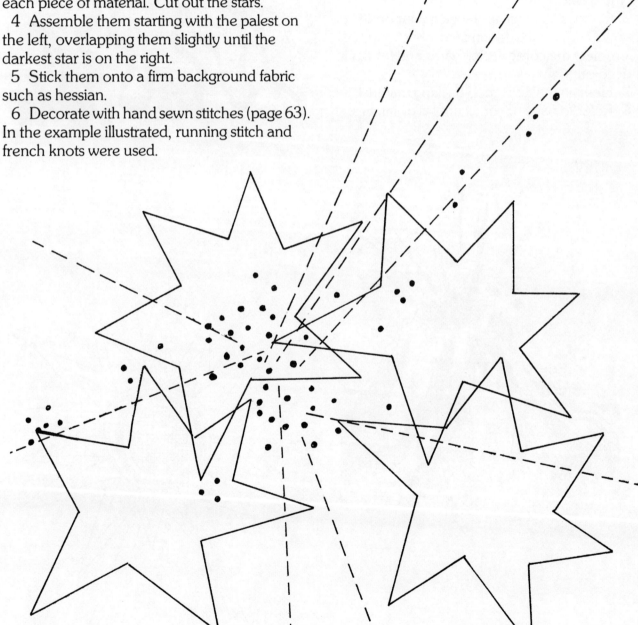

Project 3
Collage using hot colours

Working hints

1 Make a list of your ideas for a collage using hot colours. Here are a few examples to help you:
  the sun
  fire
  a volcano
  the desert

2 Choose one idea and sketch your design on paper. Transfer the design onto fabric (page 64). Complete the collage using yarns and fabrics in hot colours.

3 Hessian makes a good backing material.

4 Refer to page 63 for examples of stitches.

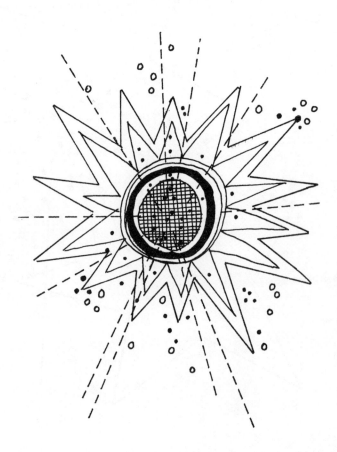

Project 4
Figure mobile

Working hints

1 Decide which of the mobiles you will make.
2 Using the basic pattern shapes on page 27 trace the pieces for a clown, a scarecrow or a pirate.
3 Draw them onto card and cut them out.
4 Collect a variety of yarns and fabrics you could use for the various characters and their clothes. The table below will give you some ideas.
5 Glue the card body pieces onto the wrong side of the fabrics you have chosen, and leave to dry.
6 Cut round the card neatly.
7 Draw in the faces with a felt tipped pen or trace from diagram on page 27.
8 Add any decorations, such as buttons or braids, by sewing/glueing them into position.
9 Create the effect of hair with suitable yarns.
10 Assemble your figure by putting split pins through the pieces in the marked places.
  You now have an interesting, colourful character, with a fair amount of mobility. Try attaching them all to a cord to create a noticeboard display.

Suggested fabrics and yarns:

	Hat	**Hair**	**Ruff**	**Shirt**	**Trousers**	**Boots**
Clown	felt	frayed hessian	lace	printed cotton	cord or denim	suede black felt
Pirate	Black felt	wool	–	striped cotton	black or navy fabric	black plastic
Scarecrow	tweed	raffia string	wool	checked cotton	denim or tweed	suede or felt

Clown, scarecrow and pirate mobiles

26

Pattern for figure mobile

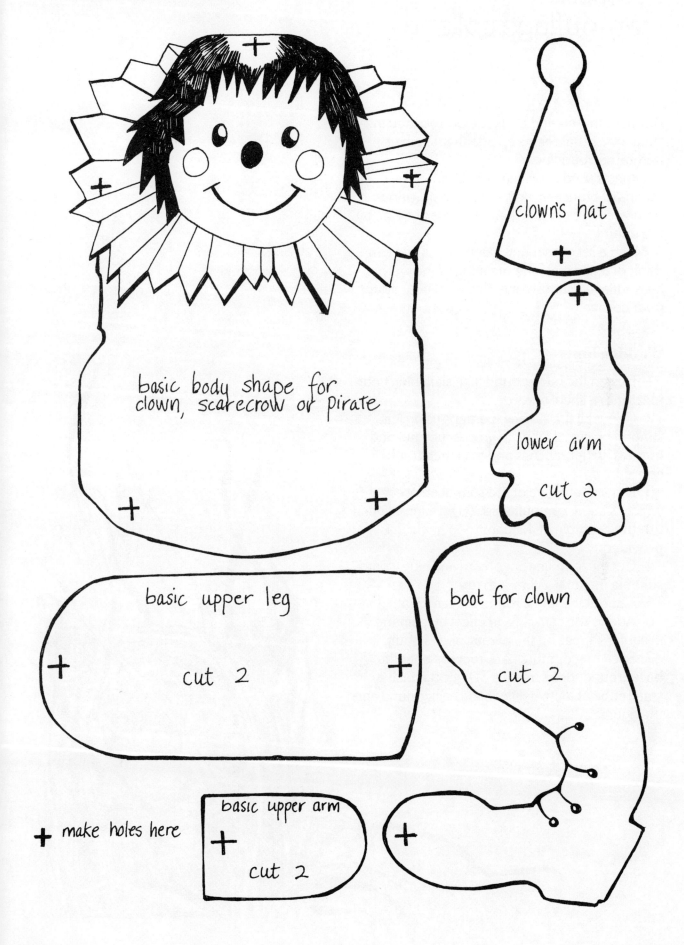

Project 5
Camouflage collage

Animals, insects and birds can be coloured in such a way that seems to hide them in their natural surroundings.

Objects used in war can be disguised by means of branches, nets and paint of various natural colours so that their outline is not seen by the enemy.

Make a list of as many examples as you can think of to illustrate the meaning of the word camouflage. Choose one idea from your list for your collage.

Working hints

1 Design the background first, sketching your idea onto a sheet of card.

2 Cover all the surface, perhaps using leaf shaped pieces of fabric in greens, yellows and browns, with branches and thick tree trunks in courduroy.

3 Draw a template of the animal or insect which is being camouflaged. As an alternative use the example of the paratrooper which is provided.

4 Cut the template out of card and glue it onto suitable material. Allow it to dry.

5 Cut out the fabric round the template.

6 Add to the camouflage effect by painting irregular shapes on the paratrooper's outfit.

7 Stick one or more paratroopers onto the background, or to create a 3D effect attach a small cube of foam between the background and the figure.

Paratrooper pattern

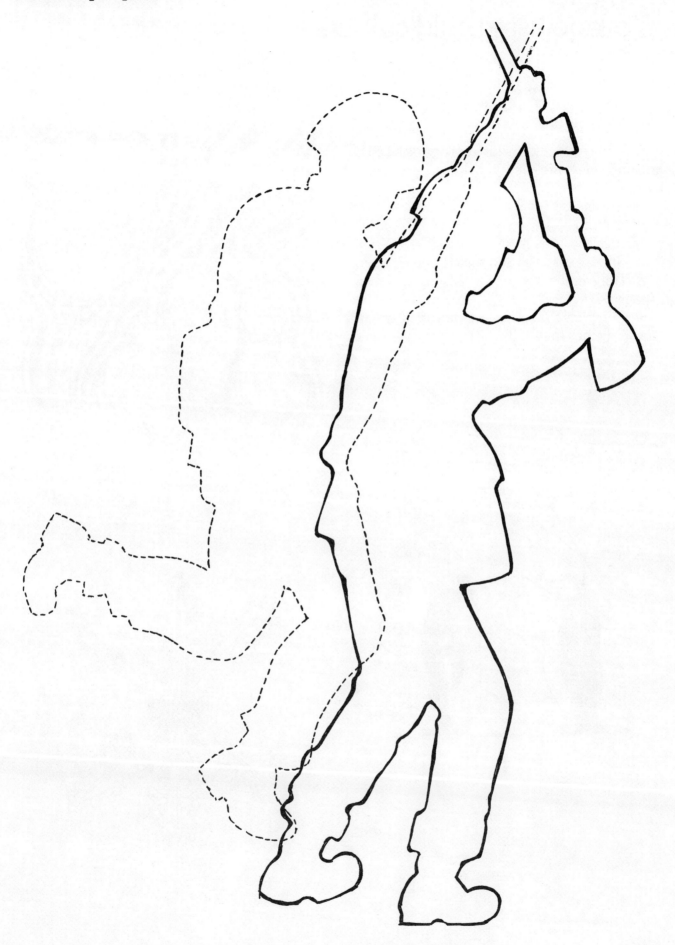

Project 6
Collage using cold colours

Working hints

1 Make a list of ideas for a collage using cold colours. Here are a few to help you:
   snow
   snow flakes
   sea storm
   icebergs

2 Choose one idea and sketch it onto paper.

3 Transfer the design to a background fabric (page 64).

4 Complete the collage using a variety of hand sewn stitches (page 63).

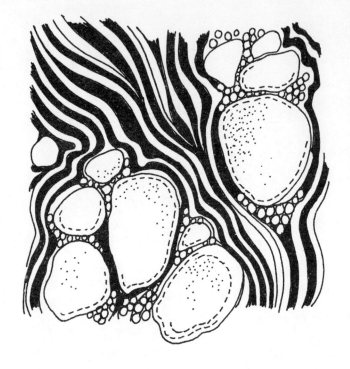

Drawn and written projects on colour

Read the chapter before answering the questions.

1 Draw out the colour circle showing the primary and secondary colours. Colour in your drawing.

2 Using the three primary colours design a patch pocket for a child's garment.

3 Put each of the following colours into a sentence.
Pink, Amber, Grey, Lemon, Lilac, Maroon.

4 What do you associate with the following colour combinations?
RED, WHITE, BLUE.
RED, AMBER, GREEN.
BLACK, WHITE.

5 Colour plays an important part in the presentation of food. Draw a large oval plate, and taking 'Summer Salad' as a title, create a design and colour it in.

6 If you look out of a window in a town setting, you may see an interesting skyline made up of chimneys, T.V. aerials, roofs of various shapes and cranes. If you looked at the same view at dusk, the colours would become duller and the shapes would be dark outlines against a lighter sky.

7 Which colours do you link with the following road signs?
NO PARKING   STOP   CATS' EYES
PEDESTRIAN CROSSING   CROSSING CODE
MOTORWAY SIGNS

8 Which colours do you associate with the four seasons? Write a paragraph to describe each season.

Crossword on colour

Copy the crossword onto paper and complete.

Across

1 The lighter tone of a colour.
4 Another word to describe colour.
5 Having no definite colour.
7 Soldiers, animals and insects hide themselves by using this.
9 The thief was caught . . . handed.
11 Red, orange, yellow, green, blue, indigo, violet.
12 A blue colour that reminds you of jeans.

Down

1 The lightness or darkness of a colour.
2 A colour linked with royal occasions.
3 The name given to the three purest colours.
6 One of the warm colours.
7 A deep red colour.
8 A word used to describe a colour which is brilliant, intense and glaring.
10 A colour made by mixing white with red.

Chapter 3
Texture

We like or dislike a fabric not only because of the way it looks, or pleases the eye, but more importantly how it feels, or pleases the sense of touch. This sense of touch is a very important part of fabric design. Fabrics which appeal to this sense seem much more attractive than those that we do not like to handle.

The word used to describe how a fabric feels is **texture**. Woollen fabric can be produced in many different textures from the very soft such as lambswool and angora, to the very rough such as Harris tweed and herdwick.

Other fabrics have their own characteristic textures
- Satin .... shiny
- Velvet .... smooth
- Denim .... coarse
- Nylon .... slippery
- Brushed cotton .. soft

The way in which fabric texture is formed depends on:

A The type of fibre that has been used to make the yarn, and whether it is a natural or man-made fibre.

Natural fibres – wool, cotton linen and silk – have their own textures. Man-made fibres such as crimplene and satin can be produced in a variety of textures depending on what is required.

All man-made fibres start as a liquid which is forced through fine holes to form long smooth filaments which look like spaghetti. These are then collected together and spun into a yarn. These are called filament yarns. Fabrics made from filament fibres are smooth and silky, for example, satin.

To produce a thicker fabric, these filaments are chopped into shorter lengths called **staple** fibres. Staple fibres are then coombed and spun to make a bulky yarn, for example thick tweed.

B The method used for making the yarn into fabric such as weaving or knitting.

There are several simple weaving patterns which give the fabric different textures.
1. **Plain weave** is the most common and used for plain shirt fabric and sheeting.
2. **Twill weave** produces a diagonal line effect on the fabric. Denim is a twillweave with a coloured warp thread and a white weft thread.

3. **Satin weave** gives the fabric a very shiny appearance, and this effect is achieved by the warp threads.
4. **Pile weave** has an extra thread put into the weft to form loops on the surface, e.g. terry towelling. If the loops are cut a much softer pile is produced, e.g. velvet and velour. Corduroy is a pile fabric but the pile forms cords running along the length of the fabric.

Knitting is a traditional method of producing fabrics either by hand or in factories by machine. Knitted garments are very popular because they are soft and pleasant to handle, and are comfortable to wear. The finished texture depends on the yarn used.

C Fabric finishes

Scientists are continually looking for new ways of treating fabrics with a special finish to create various textures and improve their appearance, e.g. cotton fabrics can be treated with caustic soda to give them a sheen. This is called mercerized cotton. Sometimes the surface is brushed and called knapped to make it fluffy. Depending on how it is held or handled, it may appear smooth or rough; light or dark, e.g. velvet.

Creating your own texture

Creative work can be made more interesting by adding texture in a variety of ways:
1. Hand-sewn stitches, e.g. french knots (page 63)
2. Brushing fabrics with a teasel to give a napped finish
3. Quilting
4. Sequins
5. Metal threads.

Experimenting with texture

Collect a variety of scrap fabrics and cut a 10 cm square from each one. Look closely at the fabric to see how it has been made from the yarn. Try some of the following ideas to change the appearance of the fabric.

   1 Pinked – use pinking shears to give the fabric a serrated edge.
   2 Frayed – pull some of the weft threads from loosely woven fabric.
   3 Brushed or coombed – use a brush, coombe or teasel to fluff up the surface of a fabric.
   4 Use a loosely woven fabric e.g. hessian or sacking, and pull out some of the weft threads.
   5 Using the same fabric, part the threads with the fingers to make holes of different sizes.

Describe in your own words what the fabric looked like after each experiment. There are further examples of how to texture yarn on page 10.

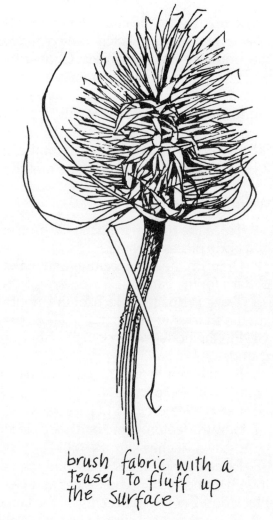

brush fabric with a teasel to fluff up the surface

Further ideas for experimenting with texture

These are all drawn examples

soft texture

bumpy texture

open texture

interwoven texture

relief texture

flat texture

Project 1
Glove puppet

Think of ideas for the character of your glove puppet animal, and sketch some of the features that could be used for its face. Choose the fabric you would use, thinking carefully about the texture of the finished puppet, e.g. white fur fabric for a polar bear, green satin for a frog.

30 cm × 30 cm fabric is needed for the body; 24 cm × 15 cm is needed for the mouth-piece.

Working hints

1 Trace the pattern from the diagram and cut two body pieces in paper.
2 Draw on the facial features and make a pattern for the ears.
3 Trace the pattern piece for the mouth and cut the shape out of paper.
4 Pin the body pieces onto the fabric and cut round.
5 Pin the mouth pattern onto red, pink or orange felt, and cut out.
6 Cut the features out of felt scraps.
7 Sew the features onto one body piece, using hand-sewn stitches.
8 Place the right sides of the body pieces together and stitch up both sides as far as the black dot, 1 cm from the edge of the fabric.
9 Fold the mouth-piece in half and place between the two body pieces at the head end.
10 Stitch all the way round the mouth-piece.
11 Turn the puppet inside out. Neaten the hand edge, if necessary, by folding the raw edge inside the puppet. Pin, tack then backstitch (see below).
12 Stitch on the ears.
13 Add whiskers, collars or manes to make your puppet as interesting as possible.

backstitch

Glove puppet pattern

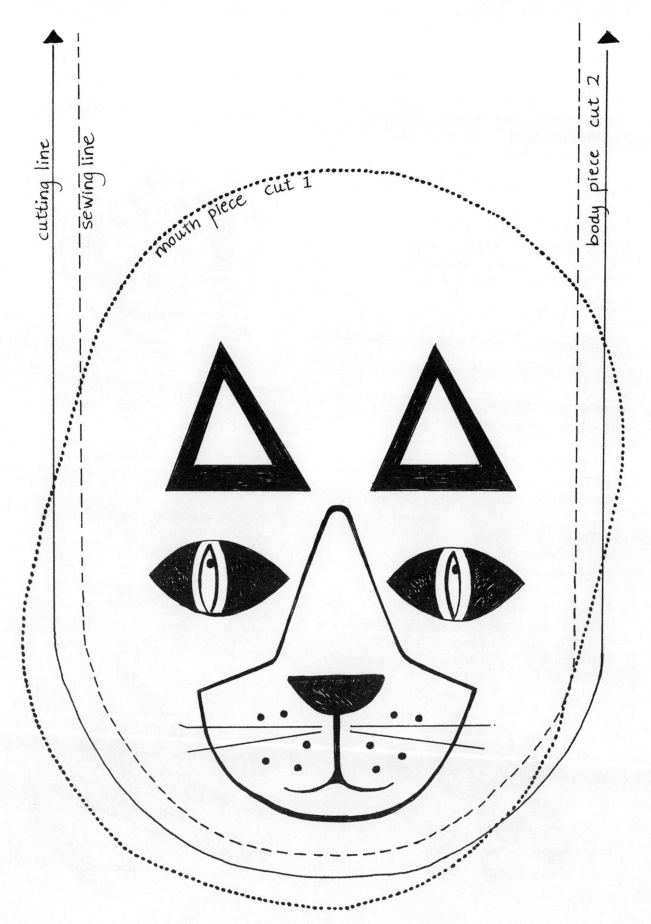

37

Project 2
A plate of food

Make a list of your favourite foods and describe how the texture of each could be shown with yarns and fabrics e.g.

    fried egg – white satin and yellow felt with the yolk stuffed before sewing

    chips – foam cut to shape and painted yellow

    tomato sauce – red felt

    spaghetti – white wool or string

Experiment yourself to make sausages, beefburgers, fish-fingers, bacon, peas and carrots.

Working hints

1 Cut two circles of paper the size of a dinner plate.

2 Design onto the paper your plate of food, showing how each item of food will be worked.

3 Cut two circles of calico, using the paper pattern.

4 Make your individual items of food (see page 39) and assemble these on the calico and stitch in position.

5 Sew the two circles of calico together, leaving a small opening for stuffing.

6 Poke some stuffing between the circles to give a padded effect.

7 Trim the edge of the plate with ric-rac braid, sewn on by hand or machine.

8 Sew or stick the plate onto a table cloth type background, e.g. a checked fabric.

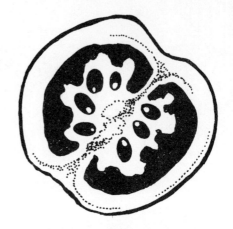

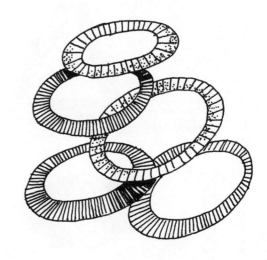

A plate of food showing suggested items and materials used

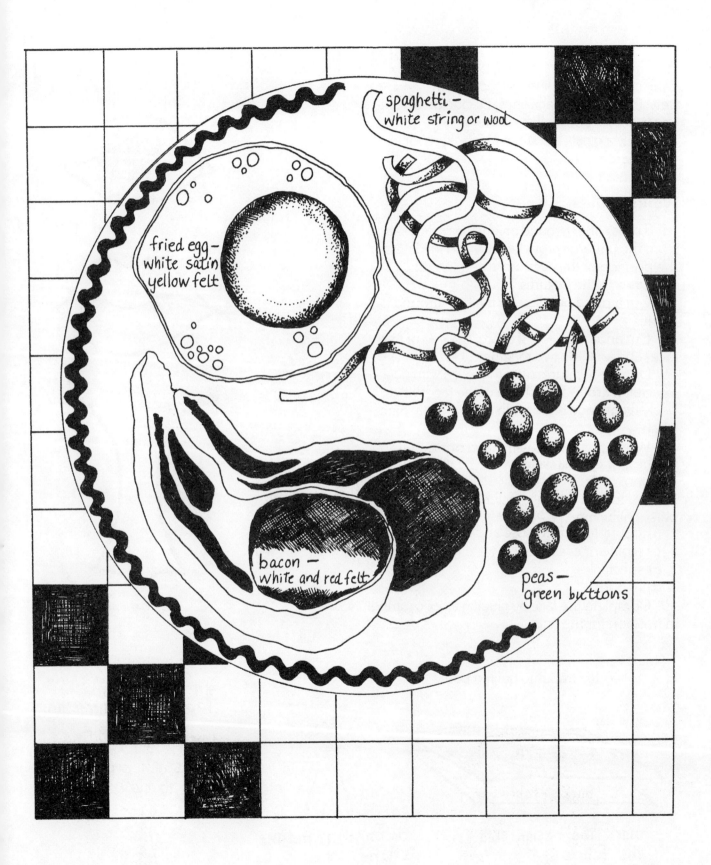

Project 3
Face collage

Collect pictures of different faces from newspapers and magazines. Decide on a character for your collage which may be a clown, a soldier, a gipsy, a cowboy, a punk, sailor or grandparent.

Working hints

1 Trace either a round or long basic face shape from the patterns provided and add the lines for the position of the eyes, nose and mouth.
2 Draw in the features.
3 Cut a piece of calico for the background fabric.
4 Cut another piece of calico, the size of the face, and tack the two together.
5 Draw the features onto the calico with pencil.
6 Stitch around the shape of the face with a backstitch (page 36) or with a zig-zag machine stitch.
7 Work the features with hand or machine stitches, or use felt which could be glued in position.
8 Try to give your character an interesting personality, e.g.
   a) trapunto quilted nose and cheeks
   b) a pipe or cigarette
   c) spectacles
   d) earings.
9 Complete the face by glueing wool or string in position for the hair.

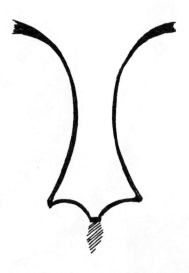

How to work a trapunto quilted nose.

mark the design onto the fabric
tack the two fabrics together

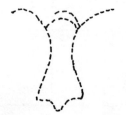

backstitch round the shape

slit the backing fabric where necessary

insert the padding

slip stitch over the slits to close them

Face collage pattern

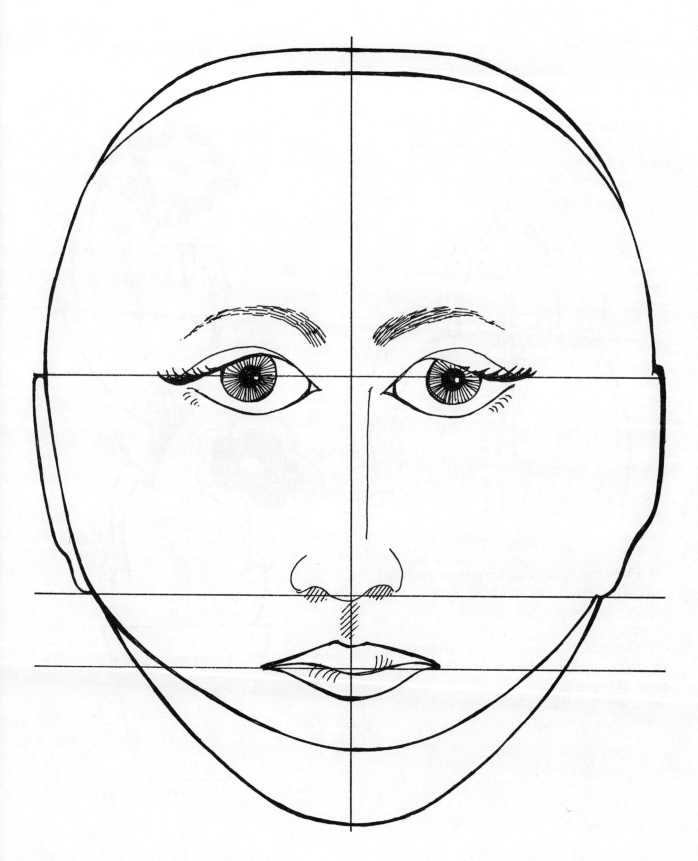

Project 4
A prickly cactus

Working hints

1 Select some green textured fabric.
2 Cut three pieces from the pattern you have chosen.
3 Follow the diagrams to pin, tack and then sew the three pieces together using backstitch (page 36).

4 Press the three sides flat so that a centre crease is formed. Backstitch along these creases to ensure a firm spine down the centre.
5 Decorate the plant by adding flowers made from felt, and prickles made from stiff cord, string or gut.
6 Stand in a small plastic plant pot when complete.

Cactus pattern

The cactus can be stuffed to make a more solid shape — this would be necessary if the shapes were to be assembled to make a large plant, also it would be necessary to gather the bottom of each shape

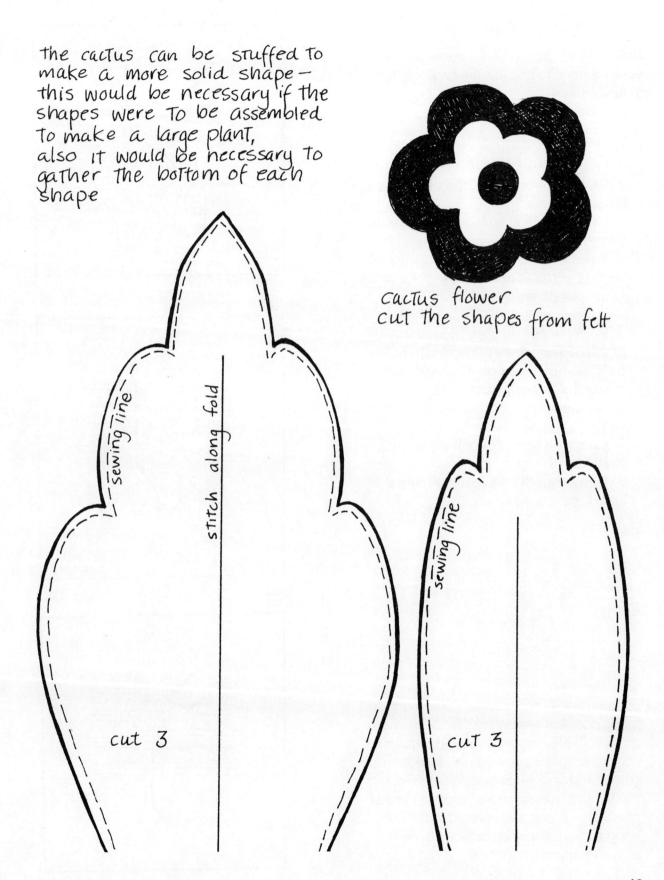

cactus flower
cut the shapes from felt

Project 5
Latchhook wall hanging

Before starting a design for a wall hanging, you will need to practise the basic stitch.
You will need
a latch hook
rug canvas
thick wool

1 Cut a piece of card 10 cm wide.
2 Wind the wool round the card several times.
3 Cut the wool at both edges of the card to make even lengths of yarn.
4 Fold one piece of wool exactly in half round the shank of the hook. The evenness of the pile depends on this fold being exactly in half.
5 Push the hook under the weft strands of the canvas where the knot is to be tied.
6 Make sure the hook is pushed well forward, so that the latch is free and open, then turn the hook slightly to the left.
7 Catch the hook through the loop of wool, and the latch will close.
9 Gently pull the two ends to make the knot firm.

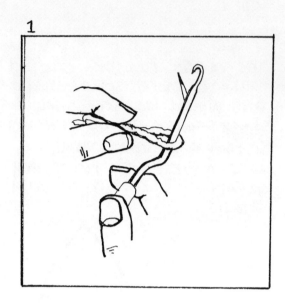

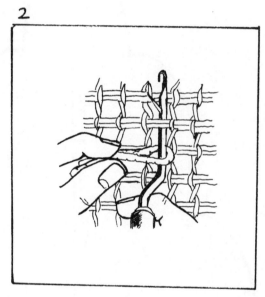

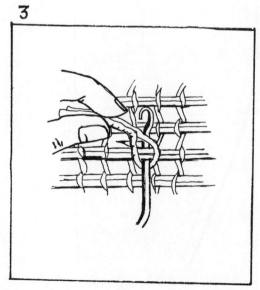

Latch hooking produces a pile effect, and many different textures can be achieved. It is not suitable for complicated designs, so choose simple shapes and think about colour and texture. Striking effects can be made from using long and short lengths of pile, which make a sculptured look. The hanging may finally be brushed in parts to create an interesting effect.

Working hints

1 Draw out your design on paper.
2 Transfer onto a piece of rug canvas.
3 Bind any cut edges of the canvas with masking tape to prevent it from fraying.
4 Start at the bottom of the canvas and work a complete row at a time. Do not work blocks of pattern or colour, but continue up the canvas a row at a time.
5 Leave a two-hole space at the edge of each row to stop the canvas from fraying.
6 When finished, turn the canvas round the edge onto the wrong side and glue down with strong PVA glue.
7 Add loops to the top to hang from a rail.
8 Add tassels to the bottom, if required.

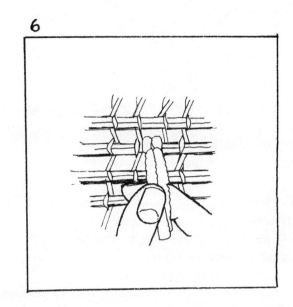

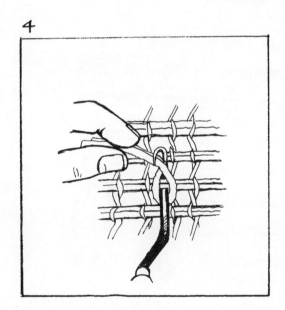

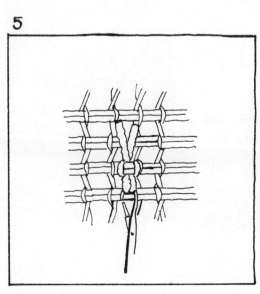

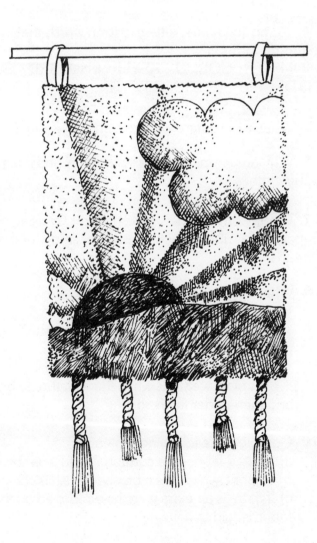

45

Drawn and written projects on texture

Read the chapter before answering the questions.

1 Describe in two or three sentences the texture of these fabrics: corduroy, satin, velvet, canvas, denim.

2 How would you describe the skin of the following animals and reptiles:
frog, lamb, cat, crocodile, bear, snake.
Write a sentence about each and try to sketch the texture.

3 Sketch a picture of a simple landscape. Use as many different kinds of line as you can, e.g. wavy lines could be used to show a ploughed field; crossed lines could show grass.

4 Re-arrange these letters to form words that describe texture in different forms:
HOMSOT   GORHU   KSYLI   EHUBSRD   SLYOGS
NKDECRLI   OPSTS   LRCUY

5 What is the difference between staple and filament yarns?

6 Why are napped fabrics suitable for bed linen, nightwear and baby-clothes.

7 Try to weave some simple patterns by using narrow strips of paper, raffia, ribbon, lace, grasses, or string for the warp and weft threads.

8 What is meant by mercerized cotton?

9 Which of the following sentences are true?
    a) Angora wool has a rough texture.
    b) Silk is the only natural filament.
    c) A plain weave is when the weft thread goes over one warp and then under the next.

10 Complete the following sentences:
    a) Knitted fabrics are comfortable to wear because they . . .
    b) A fabric which has a brushed finish is called . . .
    c) If there is an extra weft thread looped on the surface, the fabric is said to have a . . .

Crossword on texture

Copy the crossword onto paper and complete.

Across

1 A breed of sheep that has coarse wool.
4 The only natural . . . is silk.
6 A fabric with a short thick pile.
8 A type of wool that is soft to touch.
9 The word used to describe how a fabric feels.
10 In hand knitting there are rows of these.

Down

2 An example of a twill weave with a coloured warp and a white weft.
3 A smooth fabric which has a shiny finish.
5 A breed of rabbit that produces wool.
6 A smooth fabric with a thick pile.
7 A type of weave.

Chapter 4
Pattern and shape

Pattern can be described as a design in which a certain shape is repeated many times.

Our surroundings provide us with examples of pattern, and these can be either natural, e.g.
- tree bark
- shells
- pebbles

or man made, e.g.
- brick walls
- fences
- wheels

1 Natural patterns

These happen without any help from man. Patterns in nature change all the time, because there is always growth. Keep your own scrap book, containing pressed leaves, flowers or feathers, and pictures of fish, butterflies, etc. Also collect objects with interesting forms, such as shells, seed pods, driftwood and pebbles. Whenever you are designing, it is better to work from real samples. This helps to improve your ideas on colour, texture and pattern.

Landscape designs are another example of natural pattern. You can get these by sketching a country scene or from photographs. Then simplify the design by taking just the lines of sky, hills and foreground. The amount of detail that you add will depend on the type of collage.

Designs using natural forms do not need to be realistic. In fact, you should not try to make it look like the real thing. Your aim is to use threads and fabrics to produce a pleasing design, based on an idea from nature.

2 Man-made patterns

Most man-made patterns are planned as decoration, but patterns are also formed when a single object, like a roof tile is used repeatedly. Buildings with windows, roofs, chimney pots, gables and fan-lights give us a very wide variety of man-made pattern, which can be used for design work.

Experimenting with patterns

Experimenting with natural patterns

Such as a leaf – press items into ink/paint/dye then onto paper or fabric.
– using edge of item, skim ink/paint/dye from surface to fabric.

Experimenting with man-made patterns

a) Experiment with different arrangements with straight lines, made with a ruler.
b) Use simple, straight sided geometric shapes.
c) Using one of the examples above, cut it into 3 or 4 pieces, and space them out to form an interesting pattern.
d) Using a letter from the alphabet, plan a design by repeating, overlapping or reversing the shape.
e) Try dropping some paint or ink onto the middle of a piece of strong paper. Fold the paper in half, crease well then open out to find a symmetrical pattern.

Project 1
Printed table mat

First try printing with a potato onto paper.

1 Take a potato and cut it in half.
2 Cut a different geometric shape onto each half.
3 Using thick paint, print with each half of the potato onto paper. You may use a different colour for each.
4 Experiment with the shapes, using them repeatedly to build up a pattern.

When you have decided which shapes and pattern you will use, sketch the finished table mat on paper before you begin.

Working hints

1 Do not use more than 4 shapes.
2 Cut a piece of hessian 30 cm × 25 cm.
3 Draw a rough outline of the design onto the hessian with a soft pencil.
4 Spread the hessian out flat over several sheets of newspaper.
5 Take a small square of scrap felt and spread it with fabric paint or dye. For dye recipes see page 64.
6 Dab the potato onto the dye and place it on its correct position on the hessian, pressing down firmly.
7 Using a variety of shapes and colours build up your design. Remember to keep plenty of dye on the potato.
8 Fray the edges of the hessian to finish the table mat.
9 Stitch at the point where the fraying ends to stop threads pulling away. Use a zig-zag machine stitch, a decorative hand sewn stitch or blanket stitch (see below).
10 When fully dry, iron well to set the dye.

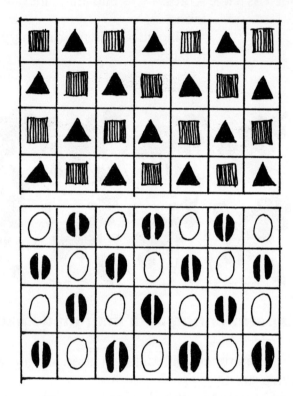

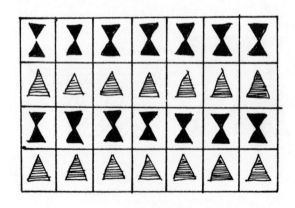

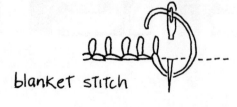

blanket stitch

How to cut a potato for printing.

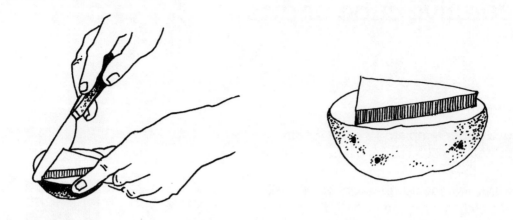

Printed table mat idea.

This is a quick and effective way of printing small objects with a single design. It could be used for T-shirts, bags and badges (see page 60).

Project 2
Decorative cube or dice

Working hints

1 Cut a paper template 12 cm × 12 cm.
2 Draw around it on paper 6 times to show the six sides of the cube. Design each face. Remember that the numbers on the opposite sides of a dice always add up to 7. Allow room round the edge of the square for a seam allowance of 1/2 cm.

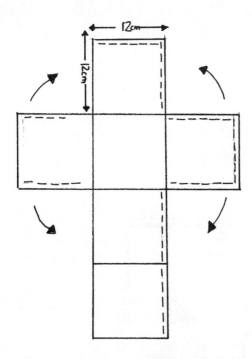

3 When you have planned your design use the template to cut 6 squares of felt or strong cotton fabric.
4 For the dice you will need 21 dots. Glue or sew them in position. For the cube decorate each face according to your design using stitches from page 63.
5 Join the squares together by first pinning, tacking then backstitching them. Leave one face open.
6 Fill with stuffing.
7 Sew down the lid.
8 The cube can be finished off neatly by blanket stitching (page 50) over each seam with embroidery thread.

Ideas for cube designs

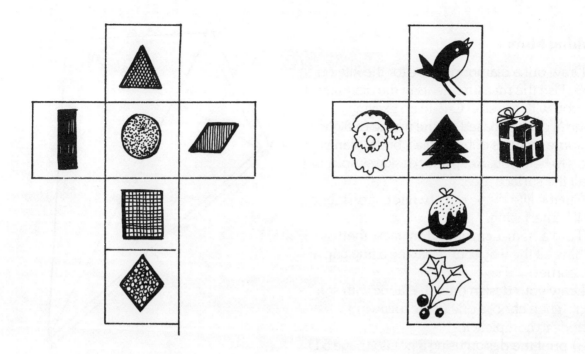

Project 3
Flying kite

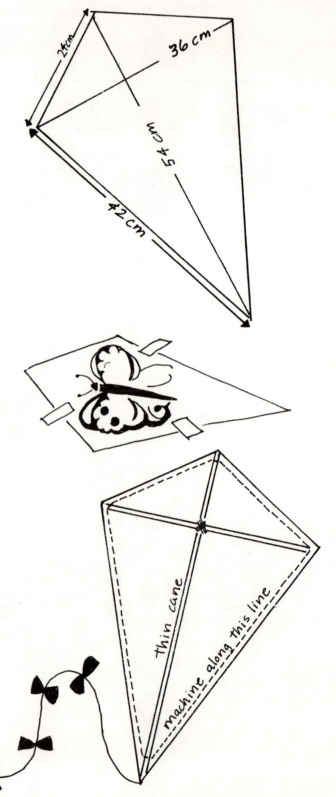

Working hints

1 Draw out a diamond shape for the kite on paper. Use the measurements in the diagram to help you with the size. Create an exciting, colourful design, based on the theme of flight. Use some pictures of butterflies, birds, planes or insects to help you. Keep your design simple, but use all the surface area.

2 Cut the kite shape out of white cotton fabric, or thick interfacing.

3 Turn a hem 1 cm wide. Pin, tack, then machine all the way round leaving a tiny gap at each corner.

4 Draw your design onto the fabric with soft pencil. Then choose one of the following methods to complete it:-

   a) print the design using a potato (page 51)
   b) paint the design onto the fabric using fabric paints or dye
   c) tack shapes of a lightweight coloured fabric onto the kite and use embroidery stitches (page 63) to hold them in position.

5 Decorate the design to make it as interesting as possible using sequins, beads or lurex threads.

6 Cut a length of cane or dowelling to go across the kite and insert the ends into the open seams at the corner. Cut another length and insert into the open seams at the top and bottom of the kite.

7 Bind the two lengths of sticks in the centre, where they cross, to hold them firmly in position.

8 Make a tail using scraps of any lightweight fabric. Tie these to a long length of ribbon, yarn or string.

9 Attach a length of string for flying the kite, or use it as a wall decoration.

Decorative ideas for a kite

Project 4
Patchwork ball

Working hints

1 Trace both the large and small pentagon shapes from the pattern provided.
2 Use the small pentagon as a template (page 64) to cut 12 pieces of stiff paper.
3 Use the large pentagon to cut 12 pieces of fabric.
4 Place the paper in the centre of the fabric shape and fold the extra fabric over the edge of the paper. Tack in position.
5 When 12 patches are ready, join 6 as shown using over sewing stitch as illustrated. This will form half the ball.

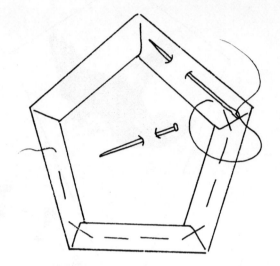

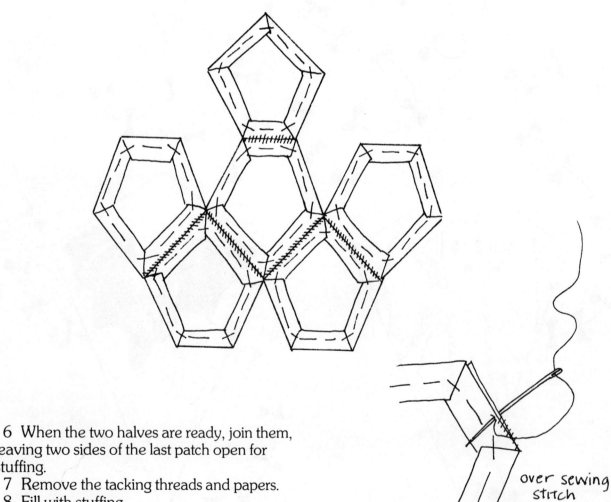

over sewing stitch

6 When the two halves are ready, join them, leaving two sides of the last patch open for stuffing.
7 Remove the tacking threads and papers.
8 Fill with stuffing.
9 Sew up the last two sides.

Pentagon pattern for a patchwork ball

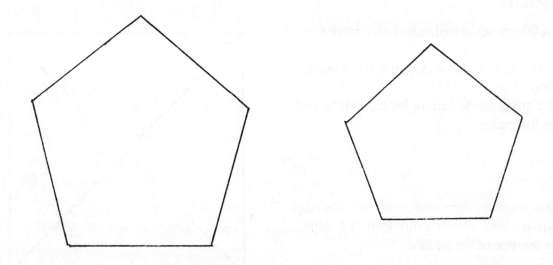

Ideas for decorating the shapes

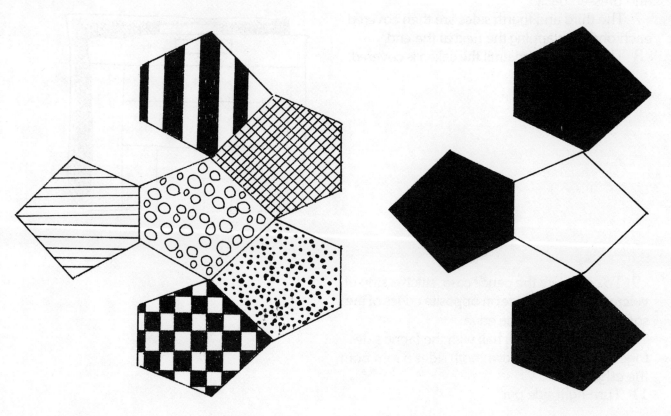

Project 5
Log-cabin patchwork pencil case

Working hints

1 Cut a 20 cm square of calico and mark the centre.
2 Cut 20 strips of cotton poplin 2.5 cm wide, 30 cm long.
3 Cut a small fabric square for the centre and tack it to the calico.

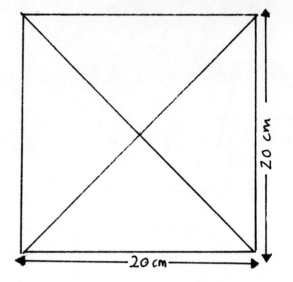

4 Place one strip, right side down, on one edge of the square and stitch it 5 mm from the edge. Cut it to the size of the square.

5 Fold back and press.
6 Another strip is stitched to the second side and pressed back.
7 The third and fourth sides are then covered, each one overlapping the next at the end.
8 This is continued until the calico is covered.

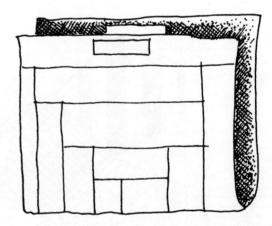

9 To complete the pencil case, stitch a strip of velcro to the calico side on opposite edges of the square, 5 mm from the edge.
10 Fold the square in half with the fabric sides together, and stitch down both sides 5 mm from the edge.
11 Turn right side out.

Log cabin patchwork

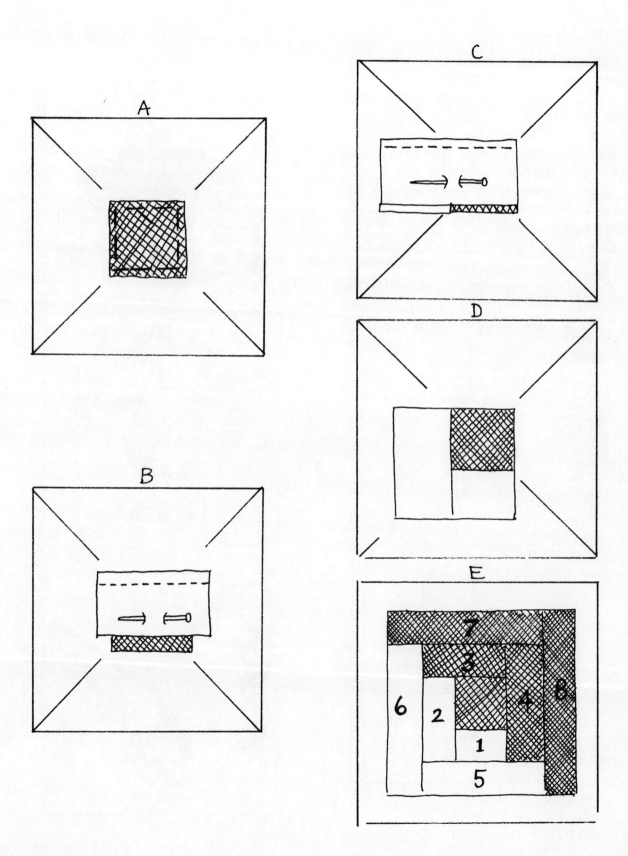

Project 6
Badges

Working hints

1 Design a badge on paper for a jacket, bag or sweater within a 10 cm square.

2 First draw the outside shape, then the motif inside. Keep the detail simple and as large as possible.

3 Label the drawing with the types of stitches to be used (page 63).

4 Cut the paper round the outside shape of the badge, and use this as a template for cutting the same shape out of felt.

5 Copy the design onto the felt using a soft pencil.

6 Work the stitches along the pencil lines being careful not to pull the thread tight, as this causes the felt to wrinkle.

Suggested logos:
  Football teams
  Pop groups
  B.M.X.
  Zodiac signs.

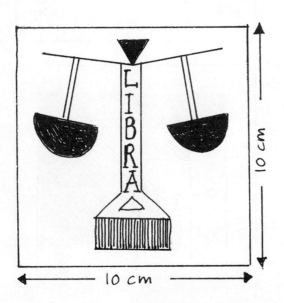

Drawn and written projects on pattern and shape

Read the chapter before answering the questions.

1 Fill in the missing words:
a square is a . . . sided shape.
a triangle is a . . . sided shape.
an octagonal is a . . . sided shape.
a hexagon is a . . . sided shape.

2 These abstract shapes all symbolise trees:

Can you think of more?

Now try to do the same thing with flowers, leaves, fish and birds.

3 Using three geometric shapes, three colours and a one-word name, design a symbol for a new range of sports goods. Draw diagrams to show how it would look on an item of clothing and also on a piece of sports equipment.

4 Some designs on fabrics are very traditional, e.g. checks, stripes, spots, tartans and some flower shapes. Create your own traditional design using no more than five colours.

5 Using simple geometric shapes it is possible to draw many man-made objects, e.g.

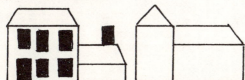

Draw a train, car, ship, motor bike or pram in a similar way.
 Make a list of objects such as bags or items of clothing on which your design could be appliqued.

6 Empty out the contents of your pencil case. Use the items as templates to create an interesting pattern.

7 Just as cowboys branded their cattle in order to identify their stock, so farmers mark their sheep with their own symbols.
 Imagine you are a farmer and design your own branding symbol.

61

Crossword on pattern and shape

Copy the crossword onto paper and complete.

Across

1 A speck or spot.
3 A shape with six faces.
5 A natural object found on the beach.
6 The basic shape of the face.
7 Different fragments of fabric cut into shapes and sewn together.
9 The home of a snail.
14 To do it again.
15 One letter from the alphabet repeated.
16 Part of a shoe.
20 A six sided figure.
21 Something that will keep cotton tidy.
22 A suit in a pack of cards.

Down

1 An item of clothing.
2 A paper shape which is used to make repeated pattern.
4 Part of a tree.
8 An eight sided figure.
10 TUNI (anagram).
11 The shape of a rainbow.
12 To choose.
13 A round object.
15 A man-made object; a form of transport.
17 An oval-shaped feature of the face.
18 A natural object that grows on a tree.
19 The sea makes patterns on this.

Chapter 5
Techniques

Simple hand sewn stitches

Here are a few simple embroidery stitches for you to try. These can be used to add interest to any of the projects in the book. Use embroidery threads and a needle with a large eye.

Running stitch – for outlines

Insert the needle in and out of the fabric. Try to keep the stitches even.

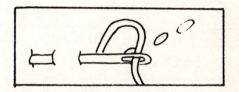

Lace running stitch – for filling spaces

Make a row of running stitches, then run a thread in a different colour in and out of them.

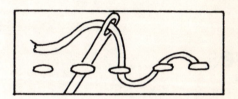

Satin stitch – for leaves and petals

A good stitch for filling in areas. Keep your stitches close together and each one parallel with the next.

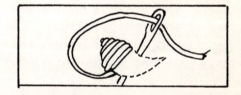

French knot – for spots, eyes, etc.

Bring the needle through the fabric, then wrap the thread round the needle point twice and draw through carefully to form a knot.

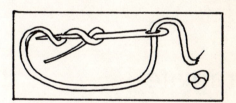

Chain stitch – for flowers, stems, etc.

Make a loop with the thread and take a stitch into the last chain and out to form a new one.

Stem stitch – for stems and outlines

Work from left to right, keeping the thread above the needle.

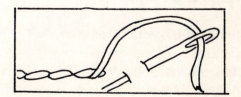

63

Transfering a design

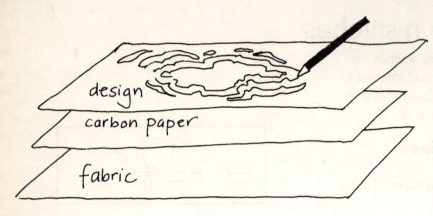

Dyes

The easiest dyes to use for printing are the pigment dyes. One type is obtainable from The Nottingham Handicraft Company.

For paper prints, emulsion paint or polycell made into a paste and coloured with ink or poster colour can be used.

Fabric paints or crayons are fixed to fabric by ironing.

Template

A template is a shape which is cut out of card. This can then be drawn around to make many similar shapes which will be exactly the same.

Suppliers

Nottingham Handicraft Company.
Dryads, Leicester.
Fleeces from the British Wool Marketing Board.
Dylon dyes obtainable from chemists and large stores.